Mediterranean Sea

Sidon

Tyre

MOUNT HERMON

Caesarea
Philippi

GOLAN HEIGHTS

Lake
Huleh

GALILEE

Chorazin

Capernaum ● Bethsaida
Tabgha

Magdala
Sepphoris ● Cana Tiberias *Sea of Galilee*

Nazareth ● Mount Tabor

VALLEY OF JEZREEL
Naim

Jordan

Sebaste

SAMARIA

Jabbok

MOUNT GERIZIM

Emmaus Jericho
● Betharamphta
JUDEA Jerusalem
● Bethany
Bethlehem ● Qumran
Herodium

WILDERNESS OF JUDEA

Dead Sea

0   20   40   60   80   miles

Jesus in His Homeland

First double page

*J*erusalem, the city toward which everything converges, is the city from which Jesus knows that he will have to leave this world to go to the Father.

Second double page

*B*efore reaching Jerusalem, Jesus had to experience the wilderness of the forty days of temptation in memory of the forty years of the wilderness of the Exodus.

Page 10

*C*rosses over Jerusalem... Toward the end of this second millennium, 1.5 billion men and women see in Jesus of Nazareth the Son of God, the savior of humankind.

Jacques Potin

Jesus in His Homeland

*Translated from the French
by Colette Joly Dees*

ORBIS BOOKS

Maryknoll, New York 10545

Graphic Design: Blandine Perrois, Isabelle Glomaud
Page Layout: Évelyne Simonin
Iconographic Research: Frédéric Mazuy

English translation copyright © 1997 by Orbis Books
Originally published as *Jésus en son pays,*
© by Bayard Éditions/Le Monde de la Bible, Paris, 1996

Published by Orbis Books, Maryknoll, New York, U.S.A.

ISBN 1-57075-143-9

Printed in France

AROUND THE YEAR 30 OF THE COMMON ERA,

*on the dusty trails which connected their villages, the inhabitants
of Galilee could see a small group of people walking by.
They were led by a man in the prime of life.*

His name, Yehoshua, was on everyone's lips: he was from Naza-reth, an insignificant small town in the hills of lower Galilee. People were intrigued, and they scrambled to see him as he went by. Was he not working wonders, giving hearing back to the deaf, releasing the tongues of the dumb, and driving out evil spirits? But he was also proclaiming a message which went straight to the hearts of the people: "Repent and believe in the good news." Twelve men, his "envoys" (apostles), walked with him as well as a number of women whom he had cured from their illnesses.

This preface may seem romanticized. But it is only the transposition of a gospel text: *"Jesus went on through cities and villages, proclaiming and bringing the good news of the kingdom of God. The twelve [apostles] were with him, as well as some women who had been cured of evil spirits and infirmities"* (Luke 8:1–2).

No other gospel text underlines so clearly the extent to which Jesus never stopped walking up and down the roads which connected the villages of Galilee to the north, of Samaria in the center, and of Judea to the south.

From time to time, the small group took a Roman road like the Via Maris, which starts in Egypt, runs along Capernaum on the shore of Lake Tiberias, and ends up in Damascus. Jesus was truly an "itinerant preacher," always anxious to bring the good news to "another town."

This is not to say that the group covered a lot of territory in these journeys: at the time of Jesus, the kingdom of Herod, which was divided among his sons, was a very small country, about the size of Massachusetts. There are no more than 150 miles from the north to the south and, at its

widest part, the country barely measures 75 miles. But what diversity we find in this "district of the universe"! Within an area of about six miles, we shift from luxuriant vegetation to the most mineral desert. A striking contrast between green Galilee, which receives as much rainfall as Tampa, and the hollow of the Dead Sea, where it practically never rains, between the fertile coastal plain and rocky and harsh Judea.

Jesus did not travel throughout the whole country, far from it. If we consider only the gospel narratives, Jesus never ventured as far as the coastal plain, except when he went to the "region around Tyre and Sidon," outside the confines of Palestine, strictly speaking. Likewise, he probably never went as far as the Negev Desert, but, on the other hand, he was very familiar with the desert south of Jericho when he had John baptize him.

THE ANNUNCIATION TO MARY

Jesus is anchored in Nazareth in Galilee. He is Jesus of Nazareth, Jesus the Nazarene, even if we are not at all sure of the meaning of the inscription which Pilate had written and put on the cross (John 19:19): "Jesus the Nazorean, the King of the Jews." There is an unparalleled bond between Jesus and this "town" of lower Galilee.

It is in that town — actually a very small town — that everything began, as we are told in the Gospel of Luke: ***"In the sixth month the angel Gabriel was sent by God to a town in Galilee called Nazareth, to a virgin engaged to a man whose name was Joseph, of the house of David. The virgin's name was Mary"*** (Luke 1:26–27).

Above

Nazareth has about seventy thousand inhabitants today. In its heart, it preciously preserves the gospel town, which is marked by the Basilica of the Annunciation.

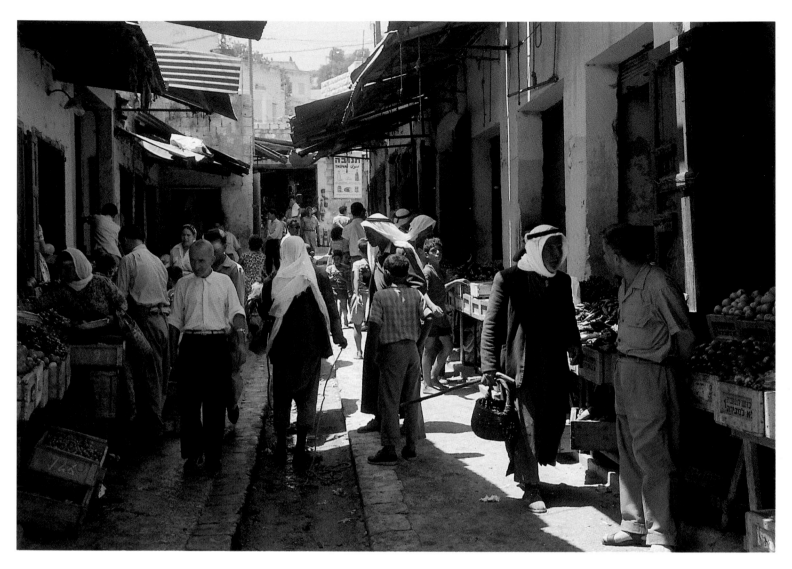

Above

No traces have been found of the synagogue where Jesus used to go. However, local tradition has located it in the midst of the open-air markets in the Arab city.

Today Nazareth has become a bustling city in whose center an important dome attracts our attention. For Christians, this dome signals the very heart of the city since the basilica shelters the place where, early on, the disciples of Jesus situated Mary's house, the house where she received the angel's visit. But here we have to close our eyes and imagine a very tiny village built upon a narrow knoll with steep slopes. Very modest houses are built of clay and straw upon these downward slopes. Some of them are just projections, with the "main dwelling" formed by a cave or, more often, by a series of caves serving as dwellings or storage places. In fact, excavations have shown that the side of the slope is full of holes, like Swiss cheese, with its silos and its cisterns.

Nazareth, which is never mentioned in the Old Testament, must have been considered as a hole in the wall by neighboring cities. This no doubt explains the disappointed comment of Nathanael, who was from nearby Cana, about Jesus: "Can anything good come out of Nazareth?" (John 1:46). The place was so insignificant that no one ever felt the need to build ramparts around it!

In Jesus' day, Nazareth was a small agricultural town with narrow winding streets. This has not changed in the maze of the modern city. Its inhabitants lived in close contact with the livestock and with the fields. Most of the work of Joseph, a carpenter, must have consisted in repairing farming tools. At the end of the town, there is a spring gushing forth (still visible today in the crypt of the Greek Orthodox Church of Saint Gabriel). There women, carrying pitchers on their heads, would come to draw water. In Nazareth, there was a synagogue (no trace of it has ever been found), which Jesus attended every sabbath day and where he often spoke. According to the evangelists, it was in that place of worship that Jesus inaugurated his life as a preacher (Luke 4:16).

If there is anything certain about Jesus' life, it is that he lived his childhood, his adolescence, and the beginning of his adult years in Nazareth. Such a town, ignored for the most part and even ridiculed, could not have invented itself. On the other hand, we should not imagine that Nazareth was totally removed from urban civilization. About three miles to the northwest was the sumptuous and newly built town of Sepphoris, the first

Above

*G*alilee has always been a privileged and an envied region, not only because of its rich soil but also because of its geographical location.

SHEPHERDS

The first ancestors of the people of Israel were wandering shepherds going from pasture to pasture with their flocks of sheep and goats. David himself had been a shepherd. Hence, it is quite natural to resort to the image of the shepherd to evoke the relationship of the Lord with his people: he is the shepherd who leads his sheep to green pastures and still waters (Ps. 23). The Messiah is going to be the good shepherd of Israel (Mic. 5:1–3, quoted by Matt. 2:6).

However, in Jesus' time, shepherds did not have a very good reputation. Rabbinic literature had drawn several lists of despised occupations, among which shepherds had a prominent place. They were thought of as dishonest most of the time. The positive image of shepherds that we find in the preaching of Jesus is definitely rare. Jesus presented himself as the good shepherd (John 10). It is significant that shepherds were the first to hear the news of the birth of the Messiah, and they were also the first to witness it (Luke 2:8–20). Thus, it is the humble and the despised who become the first.

Above

A few miles to the north of Nazareth, archeologists excavate the vestiges of Sepphoris, the first capital of Herod Antipas.

Previous double page

In the year 2000, Nazareth plans to celebrate its "native son" in a dazzling way.

Right page

A theater dug into the hill bears witness to the importance of Sepphoris during the Greco-Roman period.

capital of Herod Antipas, who was the king at the time of Jesus. How can one think that such a city, with its theater, its agora, or marketplace, its Greco-Roman monuments — which archeologists are in the process of bringing to light — did not have a certain influence on the "hamlet" of Nazareth and its inhabitants, even if it were only in terms of the economy, even if the pious Jews of Nazareth looked upon the city with some suspicion? We can imagine that the openness of Jesus to "goyim" (non-Jews) is explained by this proximity. But the brilliance of Sepphoris did not prevent the Jewish inhabitants of Nazareth from leading their own religious lives in welcoming the word of God. They were the "poor of Yahweh" for whom Mary was the model par excellence.

Let us return to the "house-cave" which tradition considers to be the place where Mary received the message of the angel Gabriel. It seems reasonable to think that the Judeo-Christians, namely, the disciples from Judaism who accepted Jesus as the Messiah, never lost sight of that place

Above

The ground of the ancient village of Nazareth is furrowed with silos and cisterns, like here, in the so-called workshop of Saint Joseph.

so sacred to them. Graffiti uncovered a few years ago on the walls of a Jewish ritual bath near the cave tend to prove it. It is very moving to read the first words of the angel written in Greek on a coat of plaster: *Khairè Maria,* that is, Greetings, Mary. Shalom, or peace, or, even better, plenitude: Shalom, Miriam.... A very precious bond with the origins, especially since some of those Judeo-Christians were members of Jesus' own family.

Today when we enter the majestic modern basilica erected on top of the original cave, at first glance we catch sight of the vestiges of the various places of worship which, from the second century until now, have enshrined the humble dwelling where a young girl received the proclamation that she would be the mother of "Emmanuel," "God-with-us."

To the left

A*ccording to Chris-tian tradition, Sepphoris is the hometown of Joachim, the father of the Virgin Mary.*

Let us add that this "Basilica of the Annunciation" is moving for us not only because of the remembrance of the past which it evokes. Modern pilgrims are more and more sensitive to the fact that, like the basilica of the Holy Sepulcher in Jerusalem and the one in Bethlehem, this basilica is the place where communities of Arab Christians, heirs to a long and complex history, come today to venerate the birthplace of "salvation history," thanks to the "yes" spoken to God by a humble young girl from the city of Nazareth. This is their parish church, that is to say, the place of remembering. In the course of his pilgrimage to the Holy Land (1964), Paul VI rightly warned: "Let us not allow these holy places to be turned into museums." Today this warning still retains its full significance.

BETHLEHEM, THE PLACE OF HIS BIRTH

The evangelists Matthew and Luke mention the birth of Jesus in Bethlehem: *"Joseph also went from the town of Nazareth in Galilee to Judea, the city of David called Bethlehem...to be registered with Mary, to whom he was engaged and who was expecting a child. While they were there, the time came for her to deliver her child...And she gave birth to her firstborn son..."* (Luke 2:4–7). *"In the time of King Herod, after Jesus was born in Bethlehem of Judea..."* (Matt. 2:1). The agreement of the two evangelists is all the more important since their narratives of the infancy of Jesus are entirely different. Both are probably referring to a very ancient common tradition, undoubtedly preserved by the Judeo-Christians, Jews who had become disciples of Jesus.

Above

The magnificent columns of the nave of the basilica go back to the Constantinian monument of the fourth century.

Left page

Bethlehem penetrates the desert of Judea like a spur. The Basilica of the Nativity stands at the eastern edge of the city.

Above

On the horizon of Bethlehem, the hollowed-out cone of the Herodium, on whose slope Herod had wished to be buried.

Right page

Since December 1995, Palestinian authorities have been in charge of Bethlehem. This event was celebrated by impressive demonstrations in the center of the city.

Bethlehem! From the most distant place from which we can see the city of Jesus' birth, our hearts leap for joy. Just a few miles to the south of Jerusalem, here we are in the middle of arid hills. In the hollow of the small valleys, there is a rustle of leaves of olive trees whose light green color stands out against the trunks of the dark yews, a subtle harmony between the countryside and a proclamation of peace.

We feel at home here. Bristling with church steeples, the city has a high percentage of Christians even though they are no longer a majority. (However, the present mayor of Bethlehem is still a Palestinian Christian, a member of the Greek Orthodox church.)

If there is a Christian feast which resonates in the depth of our hearts, it is Natalis, Christmas, the feast of the Nativity. And when pilgrims arrive in Bethlehem today, they are never alone. They are surrounded by the sounds of the hymns of their childhood, by the fluttering of remembrances of a nativity scene, by a night walk to an illuminated church. And this is well and good: it is through our hearts that Bethlehem must be first

To the left

The star with its inscription in Latin indicates, according to tradition, the place where Jesus was born.

Left page

The wilderness of Judea starts at the very gates of Bethlehem; on the horizon, we can see the Moab Mountains.

discovered. We must not forget that the city is also part of the present reality of the country: at Christmas 1994, the city was filled with lights, fir trees . . . as well as with green, black, and red flags, to underscore the recent agreements between Israelis and Palestinians.

The distance from Nazareth to Bethlehem is around seventy-five miles, or the equivalent of a week's journey, through Samaria and part of Judea. A long, harsh journey for a pregnant woman.

What was the town like at that time? We do not know, but at least we are sure that Bethlehem's surroundings have not changed much in two thousand years. And especially, in the distance, in the middle of the barren hills of the wilderness of Judea, we see a strange knoll whose summit immediately evokes the cone of a volcano: it is the Herodium, thus called because it was where King Herod built one of those palace-fortresses he scattered throughout the country to protect himself from his Jewish subjects who abhorred him. He had wanted to be buried at the foot of this semi-artificial hillock. Archeologists still have not succeeded in finding a trace of his tomb. But what a contrast! Within a few miles of each other we have the burial place of ruthless King Herod and the birthplace of the King of Peace!

To the right

Bethlehem's countryside is rapidly becoming urbanized but shepherds still let their flocks graze on the luminous hills.

Today it is difficult for us to visualize Bethlehem at the time of Jesus. Be that as it may, unlike Nazareth, the ignored town, in the eyes of the people of Israel, Bethlehem benefited from an unparalleled history: first and foremost, it is the city of King David. And this is why it also became the city of the birth of the one who was so often greeted by the title of "Son of David": "Hosanna to the Son of David," "Son of David, have mercy on me!"

In the year 6 before the common era (the probable date of the birth of Jesus), Bethlehem must have looked like a town that was richer in history than in human reality. The town was already stretching over a hill, about a half mile in length, driven like a spur into the wilderness of Judea.

The Gospel of Luke soberly states: **"And she gave birth to her first-born son and wrapped him in bands of cloth, and laid him in a manger, because there was no place for them in the inn"** (Luke 2:7).

Sober indeed! There is no mention of a cave in the gospels. In a very ancient account called the Protoevangelium of James, which is not accepted as one of the books of the Bible, a cave is expressly named: "Joseph found a cave at that very place and he had Mary enter it." We need only to stroll awhile in the neighboring countryside to imagine such a cavity hollowed out in the rock. It must have looked like the caves where shepherds still take shelter with their flocks.

This cave was already being pointed out in 215, the year when Origen, the great theologian from Alexandria, visited the holy places: "In Bethlehem, they show a cave in which he was born. This is very well-known in the region, so much so that people who do not share our faith do know that Jesus was born in a cave."

In the fourth century (under Constantine) and continuing in the fifth century (under Justinian), a grandiose basilica was erected over the venerated cave. Its center has always been the traditional site of Jesus' coming into the world. No other place has ever claimed the honor of his birth.

Ever since the beginning of their history, Christians have come to this humble rocky hollow as if attracted by a magnet.

I am especially fond of the text of an old chronicle from the time of the Crusaders (the first detachments of "Franks" under the leadership of Tancred arrived in Bethlehem in 1095). The Christian population welcomed them enthusiastically: "They saw the manger where the sweet child who made heaven and earth was laid to rest."

Thus, today's Christians follow in the same footsteps as all the early pilgrims. It is here in Bethlehem, the city of King David, the city of Jesus, the Son of David, that their history started.

Above

*J*esus often
used scenes
*from rural life in
his parables on
the kingdom of
God.*

THE SOWER WENT OUT TO SOW

The gospels do not tell us anything about the "Holy Family" going up
to Nazareth. Not a single date or circumstance. Nevertheless we are certain that Jesus spent the first thirty years of his life in that town. Doubts
have been raised about the birth of Jesus in Bethlehem, but his prolonged
presence in Nazareth has never been questioned.

Looking back, how did the life of the child, the adolescent, and then the
life of the adult man unfold? All we can do is guess.

However, without fear of being wrong, we can mention two points about
this tiny village we have described.

First of all, Jesus followed in the footsteps of Joseph, the "carpenter" of
the small town. He was known in the neighboring areas as "the son of the
carpenter" (see Mark 6:3) and he undoubtedly carried on Joseph's trade.
It means that he was close to the fields and to simple people who live

by the work of their hands, cultivating wheat and grapes. Later this experience would find a constant echo in his parables.

Jesus led the life of a Jew, faithful to the religious rites of his people. Every sabbath he went to the meeting place (the synagogue); he listened to commentaries on the Torah and, at the opportune time, he spoke in the midst of the assembly. He became aware that the word of God was within him and speaking through him. The word was the fruit of generations of listening by the chosen people: "Listen, Israel, your God is One." More-over, the pilgrimage of Jesus' family to Jerusalem has been rightly related to the "bar mitzvah" ("son of the commandment"), a rite which marks the entrance of a young twelve- or thirteen-year-old Jew into adult religious life. Jesus says significantly: "Did you not know that I must be in my Father's house?" (Luke 2:49).

It was in Nazareth — in the Galilee of the goyim, profoundly religious yet open to the outside — that Jesus grew up and matured.

Above

The Jordan flows into the Sea of Galilee through a marshy area. Bethsaida, the hometown of Peter and Andrew, was nearby.

BAR MITZVAH

The only account which the gospels have preserved for us about the youth and adolescence of Jesus is his long discussion with the teachers of the law in the Jerusalem temple on the occasion of a pilgrimage with his parents. Luke tells us that Jesus was twelve years old, no doubt with the intention of showing that he had reached adulthood: henceforth, from the religious point of view, Jesus is a responsible adult. The comparison with the "bar mitzvah" ("son of the commandment," in Aramaic) comes quite naturally. According to the Talmud, thirteen is the age of obligation to apply the precepts of Judaism. From then on, the young boy is responsible and punishable for his actions, and he is counted in the quorum necessary for prayer (minyan).

Relationships with ordinary people from the country and from the towns provide the flavor of the parables; contact with the depth of human beings who welcome the word in the humility of their hearts provide the flavor of the Beatitudes. . . .

According to tradition, when he was around thirty years old, Jesus left the hamlet of Nazareth to proclaim what would become the core of his message: "The kingdom of God has come near; repent and believe in the good news" (Mark 1:15). Prior to that, Jesus went down to the desert where he was to encounter a strange personage, John the Baptizer. A prophet for a new age, John "plunged" (this is the meaning of the word "baptize") into the Jordan as a sign of their conversion Jews who had come from all over. A strange personage indeed, John was wearing a cloak of camel's hair and a leather loincloth. Jesus went to John: "In those days Jesus came from Nazareth in Galilee and was baptized by John in the Jordan. And just as he was coming out of the water, he saw the heavens torn apart" (Mark 1:9–10).

Thus, the Jordan became the scene of a major event in the life of the Nazarene. From then on, Jesus lived with the full awareness of being sent by the Father to proclaim the kingdom of God.

At a very early date, Christian piety sought to specify the ford of the river where this baptism scene had taken place. Since the fourth century, tradition has situated it four miles to the north of the place where the Jordan disappears in the brackish waters of the Dead Sea.

An extraordinary landscape! After having twisted in hundreds of meanders, the Jordan, whose name means "the strongly descending [river]," is reaching its final stage. Its yellowish water, hollowed by eddies, flows between the willows and reeds of its banks. Nearby, the Orthodox monastery of the "Forerunner" (John the Baptist) evokes the baptism of Jesus. Before October 1917 thousands of Russian pilgrims used to come to dip the shrouds in which they would be wrapped after they died. Since the Six-Day War, the site, transformed into a mine field, has not been very accessible. Let us hope that, following the peace treaties signed between Israel and Jordan in 1994, pilgrimages will start again soon. (Once a year, Greek Orthodox already visit this site to celebrate the feast of the baptism of the Lord.) At the place where the Jordan flows out of the Sea of Galilee, a kibbutz has set up a new "site of baptism" ("Yardenit") where countless evangelical Protestant Christians come to be baptized again by plunging into the water of the river in a very moving ceremony.

Previous double page

A *bar mitzvah at the foot of the western wall.*

Left page

P*rotestant Christians being baptized at the place where the Jordan flows out of the lake.*

To the right

B *locks of salt settle on the edges of the Dead Sea.*

THE MONASTERY OF THE MEN IN WHITE

An enigmatic community, generally considered to be Essenes, used to live at the foot of a cliff, to the northwest of the Dead Sea, very close to the site where John was baptizing. They became famous in 1947 with the discovery in that year of their "monastery" and of their library in the neighboring caves, the "Dead Sea Scrolls."

Wanting to break away from the high priests of the temple of Jerusalem whom they considered as usurpers, these Essenes formed a Jewish religious group who withdrew to the wilderness to form the "Community of the Covenant" under the leadership of the "Righteous Teacher." Most of them lived as celibates, they held all things in common, they practiced the strictest observance of the law, and they sought absolute purity by means of ritual baths. Their lives were dedicated to manual work, to the study of the Torah, and to prayer.

THE QUMRAN SCROLLS

A young Bedouin's discovery in 1947 of a cave to the north of the Dead Sea containing some manuscripts shed new light on a Jewish religious movement of the common era, that of the Essenes. Some eleven caves surrendered six hundred manuscripts in Hebrew, Aramaic, and Greek. All the books of the Hebrew Bible are represented with the exception of Esther, the first book of Maccabees, and Wisdom. Most of them are fragmentary although some undamaged scrolls, like that of Isaiah, have provided a text going back to the first century B.C.E.; they are a thousand years older than the previously known texts. The books which characterize the sect, including the Rule of the Community, are of particular interest. Some points of contact between Qumran (from the name of the nearby wadi, or streambed) and the New Testament have been studied. Some have wanted to see John the Baptist, who was baptizing a few miles to the north, as a former novice of the "monastery" where purificatory washings were also practiced. However, in Qumran, these baths were repeated several times a day, whereas John baptized each person only once. Above all, John called everyone to conversion, whereas in the Essene community those who did not belong to it were excluded. We want to emphasize the fundamental difference between Jesus and Qumran: unlike the Essenes, Christ called all sinners to himself as long as they converted from the depths of their hearts.

Above

T oward the year 150 B.C.E., a community of Essenes settled on the west shore of the Dead Sea.

Above

Cave IV, very close to the buildings of the community, provided most of the fragments of the Dead Sea Scrolls.

It is fascinating that John the Baptist and the Essenes lived a short distance from one another for several years. Some have even conjectured that John had been a "novice" with the Essenes for awhile, a hypothesis which is plausible although it cannot be proven. As far as Jesus is concerned, we must emphasize the degree to which the spirit of the Community of the Covenant, which condemned sinners and even invalids, was the exact opposite of the openness of Christ, who called all people to him, beginning with sinners: "I have not come to call the righteous but sinners."

LIKE MOSES, JESUS GOES INTO THE WILDERNESS

After he was baptized by John, *"Jesus . . . returned from the Jordan and was led by the Spirit in the wilderness, where for forty days he was tempted by the devil"* (Luke 4:1–2). This is the way Saint Luke introduces this symbolic period of the life of Jesus, with the intention of showing that the man of the light victoriously confronts the "prince of darkness."

THE DESERT

The desert plays an essential role in the Bible. The desert that the Hebrews had to cross on their flight from Egypt took on a symbolic value. Thus, the desert acquired a double meaning: the place of the nuptials of God and God's people (Jer. 2:2) but also an awesome place of hunger and thirst. In short, it is a place of testing.

This same theme of the desert, a place of testing and the place of the encounter with God, is also found in the New Testament.

It is in the same spirit that John the Baptist preached in the wilderness (Matt. 3:1) and that Jesus spent forty days in solitude. He had to go through insecurity and distress in order to receive the salvation which comes from God alone. The forty days of the temptation in the desert are reminiscent of the forty years of wandering of the Hebrews as they sought the promised land. Throughout his ministry Jesus would show that he was fond of being alone to pray in the desert of the mountain.

Above

The Byzantine tradition has chosen the wilderness of Judea as the place of the temptation of Christ.

A WEDDING IN CANA

After reaching his twelfth year, a young Jew come of age is invited to "build his house, plant a vineyard, and finally to marry." Theoretically, the father looks among relatives to find a future husband for his daughter. At the juridical level, an engagement is the essential action which bonds the future spouses and their families. As of that moment, an authentic marriage contract exists.

However, that does not change anything in the daily lives of the future spouses: the young man and the young woman continue to live with their own families, without sexual relations. The engagement lasts for about one year, the necessary time for the young girl to become a woman at the psychological level.

We have very little information about the celebration of weddings at the time of the gospels. They did not seem to involve any special religious ceremony although the father of the bride pronounced a blessing.

It is remarkable that the first miracle of Jesus in Cana should occur within the context of a wedding. The nuptials of these young villagers become the "sign" of the new and eternal wedding of God with humankind.

The wilderness! It begins at the very threshold of Jerusalem, beyond the shoulder of the Mount of Olives. Not a monotonous sandy desert but instead a constantly renewed entanglement of vales and hills. Even today, in spite of the onslaught of the tentacles of Jerusalem, it has the beauty of the dawn of the world.

According to the gospels, Jesus left the river banks to go into the depths of the nearby desert, the place of purification and of face-to-face encounters with God, just as at the time of the Exodus. These forty days correspond to the forty years of wandering of the past.

Nothing in the gospels allows us to specify the "place of the temptation." Was it not primarily interior, some type of initiatory temptation? Jesus confronted and overcame the tempter. Yet, on the slope of the north cliff, which hangs over the oasis of Jericho, ever since the fourth century a Greek Orthodox monastery has commemorated the withdrawal, the fast, and the temptation of Christ.

THE "SIGN" OF WINE AT THE WEDDING IN CANA

After Jesus had stayed with John the Baptist on the shores of the Jordan, where, according to the fourth gospel, he gathered his first disciples, he went back to his small town of Nazareth. But Jesus did not stay there very long, no doubt because the "native son" was not acknowledged there as a prophet. "No prophet is accepted in the prophet's hometown" (Luke 4:24). Perhaps it was also because the village, anchored on its hill, was removed from all means of communication. Jesus went, then, to the east, toward the Sea of Galilee.

According to the Gospel of John, Jesus was on his way to disclose the meaning of his mission in the town of Cana. Along with his mother and his disciples, Jesus was invited to the wedding of two villagers. It was there that he would perform a "sign": changing water into wine. For the evangelist, this sign conveys the very meaning of the action of Jesus and it prefigures the "final hour" when he will surrender himself. These are the nuptials of God with humankind, with an overabundance of excellent wine. And Jesus himself poured the wine, before pouring the wine of his own blood at the "final hour."

At the time of Jesus, Cana must have been a fairly important town. In any case, some of its inhabitants looked with commiseration upon their neighbors of Nazareth.

Previous double page

Joy at a wedding in the small town of Cana, which has twenty-five hundred Arabic Christians out of a total population of fourteen thousand inhabitants.

Right page

At the foot of the Golan Heights, on the east shore of the lake, Byzantines memorialized the healing of a possessed man by Jesus.

Today, six miles north of Nazareth, Kefr Kenna (Cana), where there are still many Christians (Greek Orthodox and Greek and Roman Catholics), takes pride in being the place where Jesus worked his first "sign." In fact, tradition has fluctuated (the Crusaders did choose another, more accessible Cana), but in all likelihood Kefr Kenna is the site of the early tradition.

In John's gospel, we read: *"After this he went down to Capernaum with his mother, his brothers, and his disciples"* (John 2:12).

Let us read a kind of a geographical indication in these verses. To the east, a few miles from Cana, the descent toward Capernaum begins. Capernaum is a small fishing port nestled on the west shore of Lake Tiberias, or the Sea of Galilee, as the gospels usually call it. Jesus was going to make Capernaum the starting point for preaching the "good news."

THE LAKE, LIKE A GIANT SAPPHIRE

When we discover the lake from the top of the Horns of Hattin, it looks like a giant sapphire set in a jewel-case of ocher or mauve hills. It has an irregular oval shape, thirteen miles in length from north to south and eight miles wide at its broadest point. To the north, we can see the snow-capped top of Mount Hermon (9,230 feet). The water level is about seven hundred feet lower than the level of the Mediterranean Sea. The lake always was and continues to be teeming with fish, which is especially due to the presence of hot springs. Its banks are narrow except where the Jordan flows into the lake to the north and the northwest, where, adjacent to Capernaum, the small plain of Gennesaret unfolds, a plain whose fertility used to be proverbial. Because of the temperature, very hot in the summer, mild in the winter, and of the many springs, the shores of the lake have subtropical vegetation: date, lemon, and orange trees as well as grain flourish there. The wind which blows through the passes occasionally whips the waters of the lake and unleashes short but violent storms. The configuration of the area easily explains the storm which threatened to sink the disciples' boat but was calmed by Jesus.

The heart of Jesus' preaching for around three years was Lake Tiberias and, more specifically, Capernaum. Jesus was familiar with each of the small towns, much more numerous then than now, that lined the shores, although he probably never walked in the new city of Tiberias. The residents of the lakeshore, fisherfolk for the most part, became his first disciples.

A question comes to mind: what was the region like in the time of Jesus? In spite of all the natural or historical upheavals, for the most part the setting has remained the same as it was twenty centuries ago when Jesus walked along the banks of the lake. To be sure, important cities like Capernaum, Magdala, Chorazin, and Bethsaida disappeared and now are merely archeological sites that little by little surrender their secrets to researchers. But, paradoxically, the fact that nature has reclaimed its rights enables us to have a better opportunity to savor the parables which are so often inspired by such essential elements as water, rocks, the sun, and the earth. Tiberias, on the south shore of the lake, is the only important city which still remains today. Since it was built over a cemetery, Jews were not allowed to enter it because the city was considered unclean. Jesus probably never visited it. On the other hand, after the fall of Jerusalem in 70 C.E. the city became a flourishing center for Jewish studies, and the Sanhedrin settled there.

Above

*L*ake Tiberias, *known as the Sea of Galilee or the Lake of Gennesaret, is also called Kinneret because of its shape, reminiscent of a harp (*kinnor *in Hebrew).*

THE FISHERMEN OF THE LAKE

Lake Tiberias (or the Sea of Galilee) has always had an overabundance of fish, especially because of the hot springs where various species of fish swarm. Today, we still find eighteen different species, including the tilapia, "Saint Peter's fish." Seine fishing was the form of fishing most often used. The seine is a very long net which is immersed a few hundred yards from the shore and then pulled in to the bank. Fishermen also used round cast-nets weighted with lead in order to submerge them in the water and entrap the fish.

The villages along the shores are villages of fisherfolk. From them, Jesus would summon his first disciples. Peter and Andrew were from Bethsaida, to the north of the lake; James and John were from Capernaum.

It is on the basis of the fishermen's trade practiced by his first disciples that Jesus gave meaning to their mission. Jesus told Simon Peter, "Do not be afraid, from now on you will be catching people" (Luke 5:10).

Previous double page

Members of the kibbutz living on the shores of the lake continue to fish in the waters filled with fish.

Above

On the top of a hill overlooking the western bank, the Mountain of the Beatitudes is an ideal place to meditate on the "charter of the kingdom."

MAGDALA, TOWN OF MARY MAGDALENE

We would really like to find more vestiges of Magdala, a town very close to Tiberias. All that is left is a small field of excavations surrounded by a wall. Yet the ancient town of Magdala was undoubtedly located there. At the time of Jesus, it was one of the most prosperous towns of the lake. It specialized in salting fish, hence its Greek name, Tarichea, which means precisely "salted fish." Magdala owes its reputation to a certain woman who, after she had been delivered from "seven demons," followed Jesus "through cities and villages" (Luke 8:2), from Galilee to Jerusalem, where she witnessed the crucifixion and where she was the first one to see the risen Jesus. The four evangelists call her Mary of Magdala, Mary Magdalene.

Due to an increase in the water level of the lake at the beginning of our era, most of the town is now under water. Nevertheless, Franciscan archeologists, who have been working there for decades, have uncovered part of the Roman town with its two main streets at right angles, as well as a synagogue, which includes five rows of seats for the faithful.

THE LANGUAGE OF JESUS

Jesus spoke like a man from Galilee. On the religious level, he was formed by the fairly open type of Judaism (in comparison with the Judaism of Judea) which was practiced in his region and also by the Judaism of daily Galilean life. It has been said that he was "a child of the Galilean countryside who appreciated his country." This is the reason why the parables presented in the gospels often refer to agriculture, natural for a man who spent most of his early and adult years among farmers. Comparisons with nature stand out in his parables: the wheat is opposed to the weed as good is opposed to evil. Then there are references to "business matters": the shrewd tenants, the farmers gathering their crops. By using the form of a parable, a short account full of imagery based on the interests of his listeners, Jesus described the heart of his message: the reign (or the kingdom) of his Father who is in heaven. Starting with these earthy narratives, Jesus sought to express the inexpressible, to disclose a new world for his listeners and to open the door for them.

A BOAT OF THE TIME OF JESUS

Before reaching Capernaum, we cross the fertile plain of Ginossar (Gennesaret), famous today for its banana plantations and all kinds of fruit trees; this small plain is very evocative because it was one of the major sites of Jesus' preaching: *"When they [Jesus and his disciples] had crossed over, they came to land at Gennesaret..."* (Mark 6:53).

The discovery of an ancient boat, more or less contemporary with the time of Jesus, has shed unexpected light on one aspect of the lives of Jesus and his first disciples, the fishermen of the lake. In March 1986, young Israelis belonging to the kibbutz of Ginossar discovered the wreckage of a small boat which had become visible because the water level had been lowered by a drought. Brought to the kibbutz, this small craft, according to carbon 14 dating, would have been built between 50 B.C.E. and 50 C.E., and it could very well have been used for fishing or for transporting passengers and goods. Obviously, it is out of the question to connect this boat with a particular gospel episode, yet it does enable us to have a better understanding of the shape and the size of the craft used by the fishermen of the lake at the time of Jesus and, some ten years later, by Jewish warriors fighting the Romans in Magdala.

After crossing the small plain of Gennesaret, we arrive at an exquisite oasis, the site of the Seven Springs (Heptapegôn in Greek, Tabgha today in Arabic), called thus because seven sulfurous springs gush out of the ground. This is a precious site for Christian piety since a late fourth-century tradition situated several important memories of the gospel there: the miracle of the multiplication of the loaves, the promise of primacy made to Peter after the Resurrection, and the proclamation of the Beatitudes.

Many remembrances of the events in the life of Jesus and of his miracles were fixed that way by tradition — which does not prevent them from having been shifted, at times, a few hundred yards away.

This is the case with the "Mount of the Beatitudes," formerly located near the shore. However, in the thirteenth century, another tradition placed the site higher on the mountain, overlooking the lake, about three-quarters of a mile as the crow flies. From the octagonal chapel built in 1937, we discover a magnificent view. No other site is more evocative of the spirit of gentleness and tenderness of the gospel proclamation: blessed are the poor, the peacemakers, the pure in heart, those who are persecuted for the kingdom....

Left page

The pavement of the Church of the Multiplication of the Loaves on the shore of the lake is adorned by magnificent mosaics depicting the flora and the fauna of the shores of the Nile.

CAPERNAUM, "HIS HOMETOWN"

As we go north, we arrive in Capernaum. Here we move beyond evocations of the life of Jesus, even ancient ones, to reach realities described in the gospels themselves. Let us read the text of Matthew: *"Now when*

*T*his sculpture, which adorned the synagogue of Capernaum, is undoubtedly a representation of the ark containing the scroll of the Torah.

Right page

*T*his aerial view allows us to discern the main excavation sites of Capernaum: the synagogue, a section of the ancient village, and the so-called house of Saint Peter (now covered with a roof).

Jesus heard that John [the Baptist] had been arrested [by Herod Antipas], he withdrew to Galilee. He left Nazareth and made his home in Capernaum by the sea..." (Matt. 4:12–13).

The sea is the Sea of Galilee, a real inland sea. It is Lake Tiberias, or, as it is called in a very evocative way in Hebrew, Kinneret, because of its shape like a harp (*kinnor*). This port is so linked with Jesus that the evangelist Matthew calls it "his" own town: *"And after getting into a boat he crossed the sea and came to his own town"* (Matt. 9:1).

When we read the gospels, we have the impression we are breathing the effluvia of a very busy port: fishermen, boats, fish. Such is the setting for the heart of Jesus' public life: *"From that time [of his arrival in Capernaum] Jesus began to proclaim, 'Repent, for the kingdom of heaven has come near'"* (Matt. 4:17).

What was this little fishing port like at that time? When Jesus selected it as the center of his mission, probably around the year 27, the importance of the town was probably due more to its location than to the number of its inhabitants (a few thousand?). First of all, the Via Maris, the Roman road that leads from the Mediterranean to Damascus, runs alongside the

town. A milestone of the second century C.E. has been discovered during excavations. In addition, the town is located at the border between Galilee, ruled by Herod Antipas, and Perea, whose tetrarch was Philip, both sons of Herod the Great. The border location also explains the presence of a centurion and a detachment of soldiers: they formed part of the garrison. The custom house where Matthew-Levi was working is similarly justified. Jesus called the collector of taxes levied by Herod Antipas to become his disciple, and he abandoned his post. The centurion, a pagan, though not necessarily a Roman, was most likely well thought of by the Jews: he was probably sympathetic toward Judaism, and that is why the elders of the city came to Jesus to ask him to heal the soldier's servant, "for he loves our people, and it is he who built our synagogue for us" (Luke 7:5).

Today on the site of Capernaum, the impressive vestiges of the synagogue captivate visitors' eyes. However, the place of worship where Jesus spoke so often is not this magnificent monument in white limestone, which probably dates from the fourth or fifth century of the common era. The synagogue of those days must have been built with black basalt, like all the buildings of the town in this volcanic region. The synagogue is most likely under the "white synagogue," as the excavations of the Franciscan Fathers tend to demonstrate: most of the time, places of worship are built on top of the same sacred site.

People like to linger in the town of Jesus. Excavations have uncovered the street which traversed the town, starting from the lake. The houses with their walls of black basalt, poor but not destitute, were built around a central courtyard.

One of the most mysterious and moving places for a Christian is a one-room house which was evidently transformed into a place of worship as early as the second century by Christians of Jewish origin, the Judeo-Christians. Approximately 130 types of graffiti in several languages (including Latin) bear witness to profound veneration. What was the significance of that place? Why has it always been venerated? The only satisfying explanation is that this modest dwelling, transformed many times, was the "house of Peter," the house where Jesus stayed when he was in Capernaum.

Capernaum, a village of fisherfolk! Today the west shore still teems with fish, and we can easily understand why Peter and his brother Andrew, from Bethsaida (more to the north, at the place where the Jordan flows into the lake), preferred to settle in Capernaum.

Left page

*A*n open-air *museum allows us to admire a number of architectural elements of the synagogue and objects of daily life (wine presses and millstones).*

A milestone bearing the name of Emperor Hadrian proves that a Roman road ran alongside the town.

THE HOUSE

In recent years, in a Jewish section of Jerusalem, archeologists have uncovered the vestiges of sumptuous residences where the families of the high priests used to live — nothing in common with the humble dwellings found in Capernaum, on the river banks. In Capernaum's modest houses, the doors of all the rooms opened onto a central courtyard: there was no access from one room to another. The walls, made of basalt stone, were not very sturdy and could not support the weight of a vault. The roofs were not covered with tiles (excavations have not yielded any fragments) but instead with branches bound together by a sort of plastering. This makes it easier to understand the episode of the paralytic who was lowered through the roof (Mark 2:1–12).

Agriculture also appears to have been rather developed due to the proximity of the rich coastal plain of Gennesaret: this is indicated by the great number of millstones of basaltic stone in the courtyards of the houses.

The relative density of the population, the intersection of roads (including the Via Maris), the numerous cities of the western bank, all explain why Jesus chose Capernaum as the center of his preaching. From Capernaum one can reach the Jordan Valley to go to Jericho and, from there, to go to Jerusalem.

CHORAZIN, THE CURSED CITY

Previous double page

The magnificent synagogue of Capernaum, made of limestone, is certainly not the one that Jesus was familiar with. However, it seems that it was built on top of a synagogue made of basaltic stone.

From Capernaum Jesus often went to neighboring cities, in particular to Chorazin, in the middle of the hills to the north, a town built with black basaltic stone, like Capernaum. Excavations there have uncovered a very old synagogue. Chorazin was probably destroyed by an earthquake.

Jesus also went to Bethsaida, to the north of the lake. The location of this town is still debated. Bethsaida, which formed part of the tetrarchy of Philip, the brother of Herod Antipas, probably had a customs outpost. Like Capernaum, its eastern counterpart, Bethsaida, is a relatively important fishing center. It was the hometown of Peter and his brother Andrew, as well as that of Philip. It was an open area where Greek was spoken: it is there that Greeks who wished to see Jesus presented their request to Philip, who communicated their request to Andrew (John 12:21–22).

It is evident that in both towns Jesus met with failure, echoed in his lamentations over the cities of Galilee: ***"Then he began to reproach the cities in which most of his deeds of power had been done, because they did not repent. 'Woe to you, Chorazin! Woe to you, Bethsaida! For if the deeds of power done in you had been done in Tyre and Sidon, they would have repented long ago in sackcloth and ashes'"*** (Matt. 11:20–21).

THE OTHER SIDE OF THE LAKE: THE PAGAN SHORE

On the east side of the lake, the cliffs slope steeply, leaving only a narrow strip of land. The Golan plateau rises at the top. At the time of Jesus, this was "pagan territory," the land of the goyim. Ten towns flourished, the Decapolis, whose inhabitants followed Greek customs. They ate pork, an abominable food for Jews.

Nonetheless, according to the gospels, Jesus crossed the lake to go into that hostile land. Mark tells us: "They [Jesus and his disciples] came to the other side of the sea [of Galilee] to the country of the Gerasenes. And when he had stepped out of the boat, immediately a man out of the tombs with an unclean spirit met him" (Mark 5:1–2).

The miracle, which is one of the most disconcerting in the gospels, seeks to show the power of Jesus over demonic forces. The drowning of the swine — unclean animals for Jews — expresses the end of the devil's power: thanks to Jesus, this pagan region was freed from its uncleanliness.

A fascinating region. . . . In the fifth century, pilgrims started to make pilgrimages to a precise site on the east coast of the lake to evoke the memory of the gospel miracle. The site sank into oblivion until July 1970, when the tractor of a neighboring kibbutz exposed a basilica, a monastery, and a crypt where Byzantine monks had once venerated, "at that very place," the memory of the salutary presence of Jesus on the "pagan" shore of the lake.

Above

C horazin, to the north-west of the lake, refused to accept the message of Jesus, who reproached it, saying: "Woe to you, Chorazin!"

To the left

T*he upper valley of the Jordan. On the horizon, Mount Hermon (9,230 feet) with its snow-capped crests. It can be said that the Jordan is "the daughter" of Mount Hermon because the three main sources of the river are fed by the melting snow of the impressive mountain.*

Above

The apostle Peter professed his faith in Christ the Messiah in this area of Caesarea Philippi, near Baniyas, where there was a sanctuary to the god Pan.

CAESAREA PHILIPPI, AT THE HEADWATERS OF THE JORDAN

The journeys of Jesus in Galilee lasted about three years. His itinerary brought him to the villages of lower and upper Galilee, with rare and brief incursions into the region of Tyre and Sidon (healing of a woman suffering from hemorrhages) and into the Decapolis (healing of the demoniac); there were also three yearly pilgrimages to Jerusalem for Passover, Pentecost, and Tabernacles.

Jesus took another brief trip outside of Galilee, which signals an important stage in his life, namely, his passing through the region of Caesarea,

the former Paneas. Herod's son Philip had made it his capital, hence the name Caesarea Philippi in order to differentiate it from Caesarea Maritima.

A few years back, we knew nothing of Caesarea. Excavations have shown that the city had the entire range of the civic and cultural institutions of a Greek city: agora, theater, temples, and gymnasiums.

We have to situate Peter's "confession of faith" in that setting. When Jesus asked his disciples, *"Who do people say that the Son of Man is?"* Simon Peter answered, *"You are the Messiah, the Son of the living God."* Then Jesus added: *"I will give you the keys of the kingdom of heaven"* (Matt. 16:13–19).

Above

*C*ountless *springs that feed the Jordan gush forth from Mount Hermon with its everlasting snow.*

DANGERS ARE MOUNTING

The readers of the gospels soon discover that the three years of the Galilean's public life unfolded with many contrasts.

At first, great and enthusiastic crowds followed Jesus. They were captivated by the miracles he was performing and also by the depth of his teaching: "No one has ever spoken like this man." A woman in the crowd exclaimed, "Blessed are the breasts that nursed you." This is the period of the parables about the kingdom of God which, at the beginning, is only a small mustard seed, yet it is going to become a large shrub where birds will make their nests. Nevertheless, little by little, clouds loomed on the horizon. The news of the beheading of John the Baptist rang ominously. The religious authorities of Jerusalem took offense at the activity of the young prophet from Nazareth, and they subjected him to detailed investigations. A few disciples walked away from Jesus because he refused to be a nationalistic Messiah and to take up arms against the Romans.

Following the confession of Peter at Caesarea, Jesus *"began to show his disciples that he must go to Jerusalem, . . . be killed and on the third day be raised"* (Matt. 16:21).

THE "HIGH MOUNTAIN" OF THE METAMORPHOSIS

Prior to that, the path of Jesus was to lead him up a "high mountain." "Six days later, Jesus took with him Peter and James and his brother John and led them up a high mountain, by themselves." *"And he was transfigured before them, and his face shone like the sun, and his clothes became dazzling white"* (Matt. 17:2). This is certainly a central event for Matthew, Luke, and Mark. What does it mean? At the beginning of the mission of Jesus, the heavens had opened up on the shores of the Jordan and a mysterious voice had confirmed the prophet in his mission.

Now, at a dramatic crossroads, when his adversaries were tightening their nets and when Jesus himself was deliberately setting his face toward Jerusalem, the city known for killing prophets, the heavens opened up again and the voice repeated: "This is my Son, the Beloved" (Matt. 17:5). The three disciples, who, on the evening of Holy Thursday, would discover

his human face dimmed by the darkness of the night on the Mount of Olives, were the only ones who saw the dazzling face of Jesus.

A key event. But where is this "high mountain"? This green plateau, 1,843 feet high, which arises in the Valley of Jezreel in Galilee, is the place where (first in isolated booths to recall the tents of Moses and Elijah) Christians have come to venerate the memory of the "metamorphosis," as it is called by Christians from the East. In any case, in the fourth century we have the confirmed testimony of "residents" of the Holy Land, Jerome and Cyril of Jerusalem.

Above

The public life of Jesus lasted about three years. This wheat field symbolizes his mission as a sower at the time he set his face toward Jerusalem.

THE MOUNTAIN

Ancient religions have traditionally privileged mountains as places of worship. The encounter of God who comes down from heaven and of human beings who go up toward God takes place on high. During the Exodus, it was on Mount Sinai that Moses met God face to face and received the tablets of the covenant. The mountain on which Jesus was transfigured (identified with Mount Tabor) corresponds to Mount Sinai: on the mountain, the face of the Son was dazzling with divine light in the same way Moses' face was shining when he came down from the mountain. During the last days of Jesus in Jerusalem, the Mount of Olives played a major role: it was the point of departure for his triumphal entry into Jerusalem and the place where he wept over the holy city. Matthew symbolically situates the proclamation of the kingdom on a mountain (Matt. 5:1) and it is on a mountain that Jesus liked to pray in secret to his Father (Mark 6:46).

THROUGH SAMARITAN TERRITORY

Jesus "was going up" to Jerusalem, where he knew he would give his final testimony. Saint Luke describes this turning point with a memorable sentence: *"When the days drew near for him to be taken up, Jesus set his face to go to Jerusalem"* (Luke 9:51).

The time of this departure can be set during the year 29. If we accept that Jesus died on the cross on April 7, 30, we see that a certain amount of time elapsed between his leaving Galilee and his arriving in Jerusalem. It is possible to assume that during all that time, Jesus, accompanied by his closest disciples, may have stayed either in Perea (the territory beyond the Jordan) or on the western side of the river, perhaps near Samaria.

But we should not forget that Jesus' journey to the holy city was by no means his first! As a matter of fact, even if we speak only of his public life, Jesus went there every year for the three pilgrimage feasts of Passover, Pentecost, and Tabernacles. It is very important to emphasize that, like all practicing religious Jews, Jesus went faithfully to Jerusalem on the occasion of all the religious celebrations of his people.

Galileans, in fact, had the choice of two itineraries. The first went down toward the stifling valley, from the Jordan to Jericho and its palm trees, and from there up to Jerusalem by a winding road.

The other, more direct road passed through Samaritan territory. To the south of the fertile Valley of Jezreel, the hills of Samaria, which are covered with olive trees, fig trees, and vineyards, surround small valleys where Samaritans grow barley and wheat. In the heart of this region, perched on a summit, we find the main city, Sebaste, the ancient Somrôn, rebuilt by Herod the Great and transformed into a magnificent Greco-Roman city. From a distance, Jesus must have seen its streets lined with columns and the ridge of the temple of Augustus. However, it is rather unlikely that he entered that pagan city.

The enigmatic population of Samaria occupies an important place in the gospels and in the Acts of the Apostles. Why this bitter hatred, especially in Jesus' time, which separated the Samaritans from the Jews, even though they shared the same Pentateuch (the first five books of the Torah) and they both venerated the patriarch Jacob, without mentioning the tomb of Joseph?

This hatred dates far back to the time when the people of Israel were torn apart by the schism between the ten northern tribes and Jerusalem.

Previous double page

Mount Tabor has been selected by Christian tradition to evoke the transfiguration of the Lord.

Right page

From Galilee, the most direct road to Jerusalem passed through Samaria. Today four hundred Samaritans are still living on the slopes of their sacred mountain, Mount Gerizim.

Above

With its hills planted with olive trees and its small cultivated plains, Samaria is a region where Jews did not readily venture.

When the kingdom of the north collapsed under the blows of the Assyrian king, Sargon II, in 721 B.C.E., its inhabitants were driven out and replaced by five eastern tribes, which settled there with their gods. Therefore, from the point of view of the Jews, Samaritans were "bastardized," and contact with them was considered unclean: Samaria was even considered as a den of lepers to be avoided at any cost.

Apparently, Jesus complied with this custom since, when he sent his disciples on missions, he asked them to avoid Samaritan towns as well as pagan towns. However, he himself was going to brave the prohibition: he took the initiative of speaking to a Samaritan woman whose reputation was as notorious as that of her people: ***"He left Judea and started back to Galilee. But he had to go through Samaria. So he came to a Samaritan town called Sychar, near the plot of ground that Jacob had given to his son Joseph. Jacob's well was there, and Jesus, tired out by his journey, was sitting by the well..."*** (John 4:3–6).

Today "Jacob's well" is at the center of an unfinished Orthodox church. Its water is still there, as fresh and clear as it was at that noontime hour when a man tired out by his journey came to sit on the edge of the well.

His conversation with the loose Samaritan woman marked the starting point of religion in which God is no longer worshiped in temples built by human hands but instead "in spirit and in truth."

Another episode shows that on many occasions the path of Jesus crossed the path of the Samaritans. We are referring to the episode of the ten lepers, Jews and Samaritans, brothers in the same awful disease. *"On the way to Jerusalem Jesus was going through the region between Samaria and Galilee. As he entered a village, ten lepers approached him"* (Luke 17:11–19). Jesus healed them, but the Samaritan was the only one who thought of coming back to glorify God for the saving deed that was just accomplished for someone who did not belong to the chosen people. Today Palestinian Christians of Jenin have not forgotten this miracle of Jesus in their own country!

JERICHO, A LUXURIANT OASIS

At times Jesus chose to go through Jericho before going to Jerusalem. This is evidently the case with the final journey which would lead him to his death.

Above

Herod transformed the ancient Somrôn into a Greco-Roman city (Sebaste, Samaria) with a street lined with columns, an agora, and a basilica.

THE PILGRIMAGES

In the course of the three pilgrimage feasts of Passover, Pentecost, and Tabernacles (or Tents), the people of Israel celebrate the great interventions of God to liberate the chosen people. In the beginning, these three feasts were connected with the rhythm of nature: in the spring, nomadic shepherds offer to God the first-born lambs of their flock (Passover) and sedentary peasants offer the first-fruits of the barley harvest (Unleavened Bread). The Feast of Weeks (Pentecost) takes place in the summer after the wheat harvest, and the Feast of Tents occurs during the fall at the end of the gathering of fruit. In the course of the centuries, these feasts were connected with the major event in the history of Israel, namely, the liberation from Egypt. In Jesus' time, these feasts would last a week: every male Israelite was obligated to take part in them (Deut. 16:16). As a practicing Jew, Jesus certainly did not fail to go to the temple of Jerusalem for the three great pilgrimage feasts. The gospels, especially that of John, attest to his presence at the festival of Booths (John 7:10) and at the festival of the Dedication (John 10:22–23). The Passion and the death of Jesus took place in the context of the Jewish Passover. John also emphasizes that Jesus died on the cross at the hour when the paschal lamb was sacrificed.

Previous double
page

*J esus often
went through
the oasis of Jeri-
cho, where Herod
had his winter
palace built.
Jericho marks
the beginning
of the Galilean
prophet's ascent
to Jerusalem.*

To the right

*O n the east
edge of the
Mount of Olives,
Bethany was a
haven of peace
and friendship
for Jesus.*

After having spent several months in the sweltering desert of the Jordan Valley, Jesus and his disciples arrived opposite the oasis of Jericho.

Irrigated by several springs (the main one being the "fountain of Elisha," which was purified of its salty water by the prophet), the town is set in the midst of luxuriant vegetation. Everywhere there are palm trees loaded with heavy clusters of dates. The palace of King Herod the Great sparkles at the end of the oasis, opposite the outlet of a wadi with jagged banks. Herod had established his winter residence there because of the mild climate (Jericho is about thirteen hundred feet below sea level).

The town which existed at the time of Jesus must have been there, somewhere in the small modern town, very close to the ancient tell where the first town was erected some eight thousand years earlier.

The gospels relate two miracles of Jesus in the city of the palm trees: that of the tax collector, Zacchaeus, who climbed a sycamore tree to see the prophet better and whom Jesus called to salvation (Luke 19:1–10) and the miracle of the blind man, Bartimaeus, whom Jesus healed to reward him for his faith (Mark 10:46–52).

Jesus was at the edge of the oasis, on the Jerusalem side: "While Jesus and his disciples and a large crowd were leaving Jericho, Bartimaeus, son of Timaeus...." After Bartimaeus was healed, he followed Jesus in spite of the fear gripping the hearts of the crowd. *"The disciples were on the road, going up to Jerusalem and Jesus was walking ahead of them; they were amazed and those who followed were afraid"* (Mark 10:32).

GOING UP TO JERUSALEM

After having walked along Herod's palace, whose ruins are now scattered on both sides of the embanked gorge of the Wadi Qelt, Jesus and his disciples set out on the climb which leads from Jericho to Jerusalem. The difference in level is approximately four thousand feet over a distance of twelve miles.

With its steep cliffs to the west of the oasis, the scenery is very striking; it is the place where one of the temptations of Jesus in the desert was located. And we understand why Jesus chose this road open to all dangers, an ideal place for an ambush, to situate the parable of the good Samaritan:

Above

Halfway down the slope of the Mount of Olives, a Franciscan sanctuary (Dominus flevit) evokes the place where Jesus wept over Jerusalem.

"A man was going down from Jerusalem to Jericho and fell into the hands of robbers..." (Luke 10:30).

To the west, emerging from the charred hills of the Judean desert, the Mount of Olives is visible as if it is watching over the holy city. Hidden on its western slope is the small town of Bethany, a haven of peace and of friendship. There Lazarus and his two sisters, Martha and Mary, lovingly welcomed the prophet of Nazareth every time he knocked at their door.

Today's Bethany, whose Arabic name El Azariyeh recalls the name of Lazarus, is a suburb of Jerusalem. The identification of this village with the Bethany of the time of Jesus is certain, even though the gospel site must have been slightly higher, on the very slope of the Mount of Olives. The Gospel of John tells us that Bethany was situated near Jerusalem, some two miles away (John 11:18), which corresponds exactly with today's town.

From Bethany Jesus gained access to the Mount of Olives. From there, across the Kidron Valley, he was able to contemplate the new Jerusalem, magnificently rebuilt and adorned, thanks to King Herod. The temple attracted special attention. Flavius Josephus, the Jewish historian, wrote: "For strangers arriving there, from a distance, it appeared like a snow-capped mountain because, wherever it was not covered with gold, it was made of the whitest marble."

Yet, the sanctuary itself appeared in the midst of an immense esplanade with its porticos and its courts. Moreover, in the spring of the year 30, the gigantic construction projects were far from being completed. A splendid palace, also built by Herod, could be seen on the high hill to the west. The Roman procurator, Pontius Pilate, used to stay there to keep an eye on the city, especially during the three great Jewish pilgrimages. And the Passover feast was approaching. Jesus knew that he was nearing the end of his mission. Every day he would go to the temple to teach and to debate with the scribes. At nightfall, after the doors of the sanctuary had been closed, he would leave the city. At times he remained close to the ramparts, and with his disciples he slept in an olive grove at the foot of the Mount of Olives. But most of the time he would go to Bethany with the Twelve to the friendly home of Lazarus and his sisters. It was there that he was going to accomplish two prophetic gestures. After that, his route would pass through Jerusalem, the "town that kills prophets."

THE SOLEMN ENTRY OF THE MESSIANIC KING

At first Jesus' path would be triumphant. The road is easily visible. It starts from Bethany, goes through the hamlet of Bethphage, "near the Mount of Olives" (Mark 11:1). There Jesus mounted a colt, the messianic mount of the King of Peace, not a horse, the symbol of war. Thus, with the crowds shouting "Hosannah" (save us, please), the procession came down to the Kidron Valley and entered through the esplanade of the temple, now the Golden Gate, which was walled up by Moslems in the seventh century. According to an Islamic tradition, the gate will open up again only when Jesus, the son of Mary, returns for the last judgment!

Previous double page

The "Golden Gate," still walled up, marks the place where Jesus, coming from the Mount of Olives, entered the holy city during his messianic entry.

Left page

Since the thirteenth century, the way of the cross, starting with the Tower of Antonia, follows the Via Dolorosa, which ends at the Holy Sepulcher.

To the left

Coming down from the Coenaculum, and going toward Caiaphas's palace, Jesus may have followed this tiered path, belonging to Saint Peter in Gallicantu.

The second road was purifying. Following the same itinerary one more time, Jesus went up to the temple esplanade and he overturned the counters of the traders where the faithful would make their purchases before taking their offerings to the sanctuary. Jesus lashed out against them. John specifies the reason for his anger: ***"Making a whip of cords, he drove all of them out of the temple, both the sheep and the cattle.... He told those who were selling the doves, 'Take these things out of here! Stop making my Father's house a marketplace.'"*** As in the case of the Samaritan woman, Jesus always seeks to say that his Father must be worshiped "in spirit and in truth," not by way of offerings and sacrifices. Mark tells us that Jesus went back to Bethany at night.

THE DEATH OF JESUS IS DECIDED

As the feast of Passover approached, the atmosphere around Jesus became more oppressive. He frequently referred to his imminent end. He was threatened with lynching several times at the instigation of the priests. But it was not easy to capture Jesus: his small group of disciples and, we can also assume, his many sympathizers protected him. But the grip was tightening.

Two days before the Passover, the decision to eliminate Jesus was made during an informal meeting of the Sanhedrin, probably in the palace of the high priest Caiaphas. Not far from there, the procurator Pontius Pilate (his actual title was "prefect") stayed in Herod's former palace in order to avert eventual troubles. The crowd of Jewish faithful was already invading the streets and the alleys, busily preparing for the Passover feast. Roman soldiers took up their posts in the Antonia fortress, at the northwest corner of the temple esplanade, ready to intervene at the slightest unrest. From then on, everything was in place for the drama to unfold.

Left page

On Mount Zion, the Upper Room where Jesus ate his last meal with his disciples is now a Gothic-style chapel.

THE FINAL MEAL

But "before passing from this world to his Father," Jesus wanted to gather his disciples for a meal; it does not appear to have been a Passover meal, strictly speaking, according to the Jewish ritual, but rather a festive meal. Considering the gravity of the hour, it was a crucial meal nonetheless. In any case, it was a farewell meal during which Jesus instituted a new rite that would be both a living reminder of his presence in the midst of his disciples and the pledge of encounter in the world to come. For the sake of the Corinthians, twenty years later, Paul presented the first account of the "Eucharist," of thanksgiving: ***"For I received from the Lord what I also handed on to you, that the Lord Jesus on the night when he was betrayed took a loaf of bread, and when he had given thanks, he broke it and said, 'This is my body that is for you. Do this in remembrance of me.' In the same way he took the cup also . . . "*** (1 Cor. 11:23–26).

On the previous day (Wednesday), Jesus had asked two of his disciples to go into the city to prepare a room where they would celebrate the festive meal. Where was this "upper room," which Western Christians have called the Coenaculum, that is to say, the room of the evening meal?

Tradition has placed it on the high western hill, a place near the palaces of Herod and Caiaphas. Early Christians venerated the room where the

THE BURIAL

Respect for the dead is fundamental in Judaism. Before the burial, the body is cleaned and then dressed in a shroud.

Thanks to many archeological discoveries, the arrangement of tombs in Palestine is well known. There was access to a tomb through an opening that was closed by a heavy round stone up to six feet in diameter that was rolled on a groove. The dead were buried in a small circular chamber with walls hollowed by *loculi* (small places). Later, when the corpse was reduced to a skeleton, the bones were gathered and placed in stone ossuaries.

At the beginning of the common era, a new type of *loculus* appeared in the shape of a bench hollowed out in the wall; over the bench was a large rounded niche, called the *arcosolium*. The body of Jesus was probably placed in that type of tomb.

Previous double page

In the Kidron Valley, we can see the hollowed-out tombs of Jewish priestly families. Jesus walked by them on several occasions in the course of his Passion.

To the right

The Pool of Siloam, an overflow of Gihon, the only spring in Jerusalem, is the place where Jesus sent the blind man to recover his sight.

Right page

At the foot of the Mount of Olives, the Garden of Olives and the Basilica of the Agony mark the place where Jesus was arrested and the place of his agony.

apostles locked themselves up on the day of Pentecost and also the place of the last meal. According to very ancient testimonies, that hill marks the birth of the church, born of the Eucharist and of the breath of the Spirit of Pentecost.

We have to admit that today visitors are bewildered — as is often the case in holy places! The issues have been clouded by an intricate history often filled with conflict. This is true in particular of the Coenaculum because of the presence on the ground floor of a "tomb of David," claimed both by Jews and Moslems ever since the tenth century. Today the "upper room" appears in the unlikely shape of a vaulted room with ogival arches, a room that is divided in two by columns with Gothic capitals.

OLIVE TREES

Since time immemorial, along with vineyards and fig trees, olive trees have constituted the wealth of the country. According to the Bible, olive trees already existed in ancient times since, after the flood, a dove brought a freshly plucked olive leaf to Noah (Gen. 8:11). At that time, olive trees already symbolized life because their oil was used not only for nourishment but also for grooming and lighting. Olive oil was practically the only oil known to ancient people. It took on a sacred function when it became used to consecrate kings, starting with David, and priests. Strangely enough, Jesus did not speak of olive trees in his parables even though he did refer to the two other typical plants of the region, the vine and the fig tree. However, the name appears in the "Mount of Olives," located to the east of Jerusalem. Jesus often spent the night there when he was in the holy city. It is there that he was arrested by the guards of the nearby temple.

HOLY WEEK

The last days of Jesus, which would lead to his Passion, started with this meal shared on Thursday night on the western hill.

The itinerary that Jesus followed in the back and forth of the trial and the condemnation may appear complicated. Yet, even if the trial and the death of the prophet of Nazareth had left only minimal vestiges in his-tory — the Galilean was not really known in Jerusalem — we should not forget that, from the first generations of Christians, disciples have always been passionately interested in locating the place of Jesus' final days. This is because Christian faith is rooted in the conviction that a man died and was raised up at a specific time and place, on the eve of the Jew-ish Passover, in the setting of a city that was expanded and remodeled by Herod.

Unfortunately, about 140 years later, this wonder disappeared following the first Jewish revolt (66–70). Roman soldiers tossed torches into the temple, which went up in flames.

More serious still, after a second revolt (132–135), the whole city was to sink into disaster. A revolt led by a Jewish partisan, Simon Bar Kochba (Simon, son of the Star), that had ended with the victorious capture of Jerusalem unleashed the ire of Rome. Emperor Hadrian swore he would put an end to the rebellious city: he leveled the area to show the death of the old city, and he built a new city, to which he gave a Latin name, Aelia Capitolina.

Was it the end of Jerusalem? One might have believed that. Yet, at that time (around 135?), a precarious community of Jews, disciples of Jesus, had not forgotten that a man, whom they had recognized as the Messiah, had passed through their city. They were going to recreate the geography of their hearts and their memories. Thanks to the advances of archeology and historical research, today it is easier for us to follow the prophet's itinerary in the holy city during the final days which led him to the hill of Golgotha and to the tomb of the Resurrection.

Now let us follow the path of Jesus from the "upper room," as histori-ans have been able to reconstruct it, by following, in part, the traces of tradition.

The meal had ended. Judas unmasked himself and went to collect his pay for his betrayal. Jesus had chosen to spend that night not in Bethany but on the Mount of Olives, even closer to the city.

In the night lit up by the full moon of April, the small group went down from the upper city to the Kidron Valley. They might have taken the "tiered road" uncovered near the sanctuary of Saint Peter in Gallicantu (the cock's crow), where Christian tradition has situated the palace of Caiaphas.

The group left the city through the Water Gate, walking the streets of the old city of David, renewed by Herod. The palace of Helen of Adiabene, a queen who had converted to Judaism, and, according to some, a hippodrome were located there.

When they reached the hollow of the Kidron Valley, Jesus and his companions walked by the Hellenistic funeral monuments (third century B.C.E.) where members of the high priests' families were buried. We are still moved by these tombs today because they are practically the only monuments left of the city that Jesus knew.

At that point, the road crosses the Kidron River, whose waters, swollen by the spring rains, noisily rush down to the bottom of the valley and on to the Dead Sea. To the left we see the outline of the gigantic mass of the southeast corner of the temple esplanade, the Pinnacle.

Then Jesus and his companions entered the so-called Gethsemane property. Jesus was probably acquainted with the owner of the estate. This olive grove was certainly one of the places where he used to spend the night when he could not go to Bethany.

This olive grove would witness the agony, that is to say, the supreme battle that Jesus waged against the forces of evil, a struggle during which, at one moment, he even felt abandoned by his Father.

The gospel details of the site of the agony are discreet but precise: ***"Jesus went out with his disciples across the Kidron Valley to a place where there was a garden, which he and his disciples entered"*** (John 18:1). Here the texts distinguish various places, the place where Jesus was surrounded by his disciples, another where he walked away with Peter, James, and John (who were present at his transfiguration on the high mountain), and the place where Jesus withdrew from them "about a stone's throw away" to pray alone and where he was finally arrested.

A dark abyss in the life of Jesus. Facing the temple of God, on the other side of the Kidron, Jesus lived the painful experience of the apparent absence of the Father: ***"My Father, if it is possible, let this cup pass away from me; yet not what I want but what you want"*** (Matt. 26:39).

A modern church, the Basilica of the Agony (the Church of All Nations), seeks to evoke the dereliction of the Son of Man. The interior of the church is sparingly lit by alabaster stained-glass windows. The sanctuary is built around a rocky bench that emerges in front of the main altar: it is the "rock of the agony," where Jesus fell to his knees in prayer, begging his Father not to forsake him: ***"Father, if you are willing,***

remove this cup from me; yet, not my will but yours be done" (Luke 22:42).

This was the hour of Jesus' utmost trust, in front of the temple of God, his Father, on the other side of the valley. But it was also the hour of the betrayal and the arrest evoked by a nearby cave. The hour of darkness.

Jesus continued to pray apart from his disciples, who were sleeping under the olive trees. Suddenly, the sounds of footsteps disrupted the spring night. It was Judas leading a small group of temple guards. As soon as he arrived, he walked up to Jesus and called him: *" 'Rabbi!' and kissed him. Then they laid hands on him and arrested him"* (Mark 14:43–46).

INTERROGATION IN THE PALACE

Jesus, tied up, was taken to the palace of Caiaphas for questioning. According to a tradition of the fourth century, the palace was located either on top of Mount Zion or on the slope leading to the Tyropoeon Valley (now Saint Peter in Gallicantu). In any case, Jesus was taken to this high hill, later a focal point for the memories of the early church.

Thus, in order to go down from the Garden of Olives, the prisoner would have taken the same path he had walked the previous night, once again crossing the Kidron Valley, then going up to the upper city by the "tiered road" (or another parallel path), which we mentioned earlier.

Above

A model, as precise as possible, depicts the city at the time of Herod. In the foreground, the grandiose mass of the court surrounding the temple.

To the left

The western wall (the "wailing" wall), an important place of Jewish piety, corresponds to the southwest foundation of the esplanade expanded by Herod. It is the site of festivals and prayers that celebrate all the great moments of the religious and political life of Israel.

The trial of Jesus before the former high priest Annas, then before his son-in-law, Caiaphas, the current high priest, is one of the most debated episodes of the Passion of Jesus. The evangelist John does not even mention it. Moreover, such a trial presents the crucial problem of the authority of the Jewish high priest at the time to administer the death penalty.

No reliable trace of the palace of Caiaphas has been found. We can resort only to a rather vague tradition of the fourth century (the journey of a pilgrim from Bordeaux in 333). Nevertheless, the testimony of the earliest Christian travelers tends to locate this palace at the present place of Saint Peter in Gallicantu and not a few hundred yards higher on Mount Zion in the Armenian Patriarchate.

The name of the church "of the crowing cock" (Gallicantu) alludes to the denial of the prince of the apostles: ***"At that moment, while he was still speaking, the cock crowed. The Lord turned and looked at Peter. Then Peter remembered the word of the Lord, how he had said to him, 'Before the cock crows today, you will deny me three times.' And he went out and wept bitterly"*** (Luke 22:60–62).

Throughout the night, Jesus would undergo interrogations, first by Annas, then by Caiaphas. To Caiaphas's question: "Are you the Messiah, the Son of the Blessed One?" the accused answered: ***"I am and you will see the Son of Man seated at the right hand of the Power and coming with the clouds of heaven."*** At that point, the high priest tore his clothes and said: "You have heard the blasphemy. What is your decision?" All of them responded that Jesus deserved death (Mark 14:55–61).

Wherever the authentic location of the palace might be, the Church of Saint Peter in Gallicantu is certainly evocative for us. Excavations have shown that under Byzantine domination (fourth to seventh centuries) a Jewish ritual bath was the object of Christian veneration. Carved or red and black painted crosses still preserve that memory. Later on, pious Christians regarded this hole in the ground (the bath) as the place where Peter wept after his denial, indeed the place in the palace of Caiaphas where Christ might have spent the night of his trial.

"HE SUFFERED UNDER PONTIUS PILATE"

The day had just dawned. The servants of the high priest took Jesus to the "praetorium" of Pontius Pilate, the Roman governor, a few hundred yards away. Herod's palace was nearby, to the north but on the same hill. It is in the "upper city," precisely in the old royal palace where Pilate set

Right page

The humble and beautiful "Anastasis" (the Basilica of the Resurrection) goes back, in its present state, to the Crusades. The same monument includes the sites of the death (summit of calvary) and the Resurrection of the Lord (under the dome).

up his tribunal (his "praetorium"): as a matter of fact, tradition demanded that the representative of Roman authority should sit in the very place where the old law was administered. This sumptuous palace was also a fortress, defended by three towers. The foundations of one of these towers, the Phasael Tower, can still be seen today in the "Tower of David," near the Jaffa Gate.

When Pontius Pilate, the "prefect," came up from the port of Caesarea, his habitual place of residence, he did not think that he would have to judge an obscure Galilean prophet and that, paradoxically, this trial would make him forever famous. Flavius Josephus tells us that Pilate was a cruel and inflexible man. In addition, he was deeply anti-Semitic.

During the first hours of the morning, the prisoner was handed over to the governor's guards. Pilate was intrigued by the Galilean. But since he did not know what to make of Jesus' answers, he uttered the phrase "What is truth?" Then it occurred to him to have Jesus tried before King Herod Antipas, who was staying in Jerusalem for the Passover feast. Antipas, the tetrarch of Galilee, was indeed the king of Jesus.

Saint Luke relates this episode for us. The procession started off again with Jesus still bound. The Hasmonaean Palace, where Antipas was residing, was located in the now filled-up Tyropoeon Valley, very close to the temple. When Jesus remained silent in the presence of the man he had once called "a fox," the only thing left to do was to send Jesus back to Pilate — after dressing him in a cloak to mock him.

According to Saint Luke, who was writing for "pagans," Pilate, who was ideologically opposed to the Jews, attempted by all sorts of ways to deny them their prey. He gave them the choice between releasing a bandit, Barabbas, or Jesus. For the sake of peace and quiet, ***"Pilate, wishing to satisfy the crowd, released Barabbas for them; and after flogging Jesus, he handed him over to be crucified"*** (Mark 15:15).

TO GOLGOTHA, THE PLACE OF THE SKULL

Carrying the patibulum, the transversal bar of the cross on which he would be nailed, Jesus, weakened by the scourging and the crown of thorns, walked heavily to the hill of Golgotha, a place near the city where those condemned to death were executed. It was customary to have the condemned paraded through the streets of the city to impress bystanders. After walking about five hundred yards, the procession went out through the north gate, which no longer exists. (This Ephraim Gate is probably the

gate of which some vestiges have been discovered in the Russian Alexander Hospice, located very close to the Basilica of the Holy Sepulcher.)

The knoll of Golgotha emerges right away, blocking the horizon. It was an old quarry that had been transformed into a garden: *"Now there was a garden in the place where he was crucified and in the garden there was a new tomb"* (John 19:41). On top of the hill a barren and smooth surface emerged that formed a kind of cranial cap, hence the Hebrew name of *golgotha,* the skull, or *calvarium* in the Latin transcription. This rocky peak where the cross was placed can be clearly seen today from the Church of the Holy Sepulcher, since the side of the rock and its summit were cleared away a few years ago.

The gospels are very discreet about the torture. A single sentence suffices: *"It was nine o'clock in the morning when they crucified him . . . and with him they crucified two bandits"* (Mark 15:25–27). Since the hill of Golgotha is very close to the wall, many bystanders came to see the execution, and they mocked the Galilean who, after he had saved others, "cannot save himself." The crucified one desperately attempted to breathe. With each passing minute, he sank down a little more. People who are crucified die of asphyxiation.

The mockery of the passersby struck a cruel blow to the hearts of the few friends of Jesus, especially the women who had not run away but who watched from a distance. Their names vary according to the gospels. Only one of them is identified by three evangelists: Mary of Magdala. She would also be among the women who looked inside the tomb of Jesus and found it empty on the third day. Finally, according to John, she is the one to whom the risen Jesus would first appear. On the other hand, John is the only evangelist who draws our attention to the presence of Mary, the mother of Jesus, at the foot of the cross.

"Standing near the cross of Jesus were his mother and his mother's sister, Mary, the wife of Clopas and Mary Magdalene. When Jesus saw his mother and the disciple whom he loved standing beside her, he said to his mother: 'Woman, here is your son.' Then he said to the disciple, 'Here is your mother.' And from that hour the disciple took her into his own home" (John 19:25–27).

It was three o'clock in the afternoon. The torture of the cross had lasted six hours. Suddenly *"Jesus gave a loud cry and he breathed his last"* (Mark 15:37). It was the eve of the sabbath, therefore a Friday. John specifies that this "sabbath was a day of great solemnity" because the Passover occurred on a sabbath that year. In all likelihood, this was April 7 in the year 30. The crucified one was approximately thirty-three years old.

Left page

G roups of pilgrims customarily carry a wooden cross to the Holy Sepulcher, the site of Calvary and of the tomb, of the death and the Resurrection.

THE BURIAL IN A NEW TOMB

The summit of Golgotha was bathed in diffused light. It was dusk. The bystanders had scattered in order to prepare for the Passover. The women were the only ones remaining there. They approached the foot of the cross. In turn, encouraged by the darkness, the disciples must have come forward. They were overwhelmed before the bloody corpse of the man they had admired and loved and in whom they had believed, the Messiah of God.

At that point, Joseph of Arimathea intervened. He "was a disciple of Jesus, though a secret one because of his fear of the Jews" (John 19:38). He was a member of the Sanhedrin, undoubtedly a prominent man and a landowner. With courage, he went to Pilate to ask him for "the body of Jesus." The Roman, who was surprised to learn that the crucified one had already died, granted his request.

It so happened that Joseph already had a tomb in which no member of his family had yet been laid. That tomb was very close to the place of the crucifixion but in a garden that was part of a private estate. In fact, the tomb was hewn in a vertical side of a former quarry, about fifty yards from the place of the crucifixion.

"Now there was a garden in the place where he was crucified and in the garden there was a new tomb in which no one had been laid. And so, because it was the Jewish Day of Preparation and the tomb was nearby, they laid Jesus there" (John 19:41–42).

Other prominent people had also used the same hewn sides, left from the quarries, for their family tombs. In fact, in the Basilica of the Holy Sepulcher, near the place of the tomb of Jesus, there are other tombs of the same type. They consist of a simple stone bench with a large rounded niche above. The sepulcher where the body of Jesus was placed must have been like that. The door was low: Simon Peter had to bend down to look inside (John 20:5). A heavy stone that had to be rolled away closed the tomb (Mark 16:3). Outside, to the right, there was a small bench where, two days later, the women would see "a young man . . . sitting on the right side" (Mark 16:5).

Thus, within about ten yards of each other we have the place of the crucifixion and the tomb of the prophet from Galilee. From a human point of view, it seemed that his adventure was really going to end on the hill of the Skull, on Calvary. Jesus' friends had gone back to the city after having looked one last time at the round stone that sealed the tomb.

Right page

During the liturgical time of the Passion, Christians reenact the symbolic gestures of Jesus: here we have the washing of feet by an Orthodox priest.

To the left

"Christ has risen." "He has truly risen." This is the greeting of Easter morning in Orthodox countries. In the Basilica of the Anastasis, at dawn, the torch of the paschal light, the symbol of life, is passed from one member of the congregation to another.

In other words, Jesus' death on the cross seems to have shattered the enthusiasm which had prompted the disciples to follow him on the roads of Galilee, of Samaria, and of the desert. As the two disciples, on their way to Emmaus, said at that moment, "But we had hoped that he was the one to redeem Israel" (Luke 24:21). Did not the death of the man in whom they had believed prove that God had not acknowledged him as the Messiah? A mere prophet like the others.

All they had left were the memories of their three-year companionship. Memories of enthusiasm but also of cowardice. Unlike the women, the disciples had not shown a great deal of bravery. And Peter, their leader, had even denied Jesus three times.

THE EMPTY TOMB

It was then that a cry burst forth from the distraught community of the disciples. Greeted with disbelief at first, it gradually gained more ground as others went in to see: "The tomb is empty. He is not here!"

The discovery of the empty tomb, shared by the four evangelists, opens the way to another seemingly senseless statement: he has risen, that is to say, he has been raised from the dead. Let us reread the testimony of Mark: *"When the sabbath was over, Mary of Magdalene, and Mary the mother of James, and Salome bought spices, so that they might go and anoint him.... As they entered the tomb, they saw a young man, dressed in a white robe, sitting on the right side; and they were alarmed. But he said to them, 'Do not be alarmed; you are looking for Jesus of Nazareth who was crucified. He has been raised; he is not here.... There is the place where they laid him. But go, tell his disciples and Peter that he is going ahead of you to Galilee'"* (Mark 16:1–7).

Hearing the women's report, Peter and John themselves went to the tomb: *"Then Peter and the other disciple [the one whom Jesus loved] set out and went toward the tomb. The two were running together, but the other disciple outran Peter and reached the tomb first. He bent down to look in and saw the linen wrappings lying there, but he did not go in. Then Simon Peter came, following him [the other disciple], and went into the tomb. He saw the linen wrappings lying there, and the cloth that had been on Jesus' head, not lying with the linen wrappings but rolled up in a place by itself. Then the other disciple, who reached the tomb first, also went in, and he saw and believed"* (John 20:3–8).

Empty tomb . . . However, the first appearance of the risen Lord was not to the disciples but rather to a woman, Mary of Magdala, who had

Right page

*I*nside the Holy *Sepulcher, the presence of other tombs near Jesus' tomb proves that Golgotha was outside of the city, since it was forbidden to bury the dead inside the city.*

remained standing and weeping outside the tomb. She was the one who addressed a man standing by the tomb whom she thought was the gardener. Awe-inspiring dialogue: ***"Sir, if you have carried him away, tell me where you have laid him and I will take him away. Jesus said to her, 'Miriam!' She turned and said to him in Hebrew, 'Rabbouni!' (which means Teacher)"*** (John 20:15–16).

Women played a predominant role in the Passion and the hours of waiting prior to the Resurrection. When he established the official list of Jesus' appearances in 55–56, that is to say, some twenty years after the death of Jesus, Paul of Tarsus did not mention these women. In spite of this omission, their faith permeated with love has been decisive in the proclamation of this unparalleled news: he is risen!

SITES OF THE CRUCIFIXION AND THE TOMB

After having read these accounts, Christians who arrive in Jerusalem to pray at the sites of the death and the Resurrection of Jesus are perplexed, to say the least. They come to the site which they are told is the place of the crucifixion and the tomb; in their imagination it is most likely an isolated hill situated outside the ramparts, a tomb hewn in the rock and a garden filled with trees. And they find themselves in front of a church which is not only full of labyrinths and dark recesses but also surrounded by convents. And in addition, it is right in the middle of the city!

And yet, paradoxically, all of this speaks for this holy place. Some eleven years after the death of Jesus, Golgotha, with its two precious memories, ceased to rise outside the walls. Under Agrippa I (from 41 to 44), a new wall enclosed it within the perimeter of the city. Worse still, in 135, when Hadrian destroyed Jerusalem to replace it with the Roman city Aelia Capitolina, the site of Golgotha was reserved for the forum and a temple to Venus was erected there. As a result, construction to fill in the area concealed the original sites. Yet, the Judeo-Christian community, back in the holy city after a short while, could not easily forget the location of the two venerated sites.

Then, at the beginning of the fourth century, the unexpected happened. By the Edict of Milan, Emperor Constantine granted freedom of worship to Christians. In 325, he decided to have a basilica built in Jerusalem, and this is why these two sites have been located right in the heart of the city for centuries. In spite of the scars of history, fires, and depredations, the two sites of the cross and the tomb are still there, and they can be understood by anyone who takes the time.

In the rock of the holy city, these sites bear witness to the fact that faith in Jesus of Nazareth, the Son of God, is the passage from death (the crucifixion) to life outside the tomb (the Resurrection). Eastern Christians are right in calling the emblematic monument the Anastasis, the Resurrection, rather than the Holy Sepulcher. The path of the Galilean did not end at the empty tomb. As he said to his disciples after his Resurrection, "he would go ahead of them to Galilee." It was there that he appeared to his disciples just as he had manifested himself to the two men on the way to Emmaus. Tradition would situate his "going up to heaven" on the Mount of Olives.

The human portion of the road of Jesus seemingly stopped in Jerusalem. But under the prompting of the Spirit, it would soon begin again from the holy city, fifty days later on the day of Pentecost. It is to the south of the holy city, on Mount Zion, that a highly venerable tradition situates the descent of the Holy Spirit. This is really the birthplace of the Christian church. Before the gathered crowd symbolizing the nations of the whole known universe, the voice of Peter rang out: ***"This man, Jesus of Nazareth, God has raised him up.... God made Lord and Christ this Jesus whom you crucified"*** (Acts 2:22, 24, 36).

Above

*O*n the summit of the Mount of Olives, in the fourth century, pious Christians built a monument in honor of the Lord's ascension into heaven.

TABLE OF CONTENTS

PHOTO CREDITS

Pages 120–122

The three monotheistic religions stemming from Abraham, their father in the faith, consider Jerusalem as a holy city. For the Jews, it is the city of David, and for the Israelis it is the eternal capital of Israel at the political level.

Pages 123–125

Jerusalem, the holy city of Christians. For them who no longer claim possession of the city as Christians, it is primarily the city where Jesus gave his final testimony, the symbol of the heavenly Jerusalem.

Pages 126–127

Islam also considers Jerusalem (El Quds, "the holiness") as a sacred city. It was from the holy city that Mohammed accomplished his night journey to the seventh heaven.